by Spencer Brinker

Consultant:
Beth Gambro
Reading Specialist
Yorkville, Illinois

Contents

BEARPORT
PUBLISHING

New York, New York

At Home

Where am I?
I am at home!

What do I spy?

I spy a chair.

It is yellow.

I spy a table.

It is big.

I spy a rug.

It is round.

I spy a couch.

It is blue.

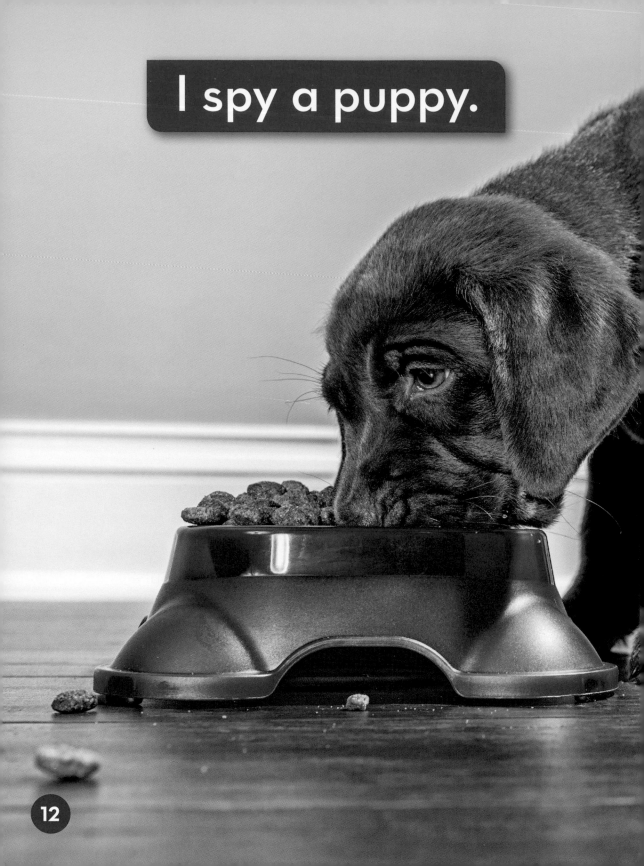

I spy a puppy.

It is brown.

I spy a family, too!

They are smiling.

Key Words

chair

couch

puppy

rug

table

Index

About the Author

Spencer Brinker lives and works in New York City. In such a big city, you can spy almost anything.

Teaching Tips

Before Reading

✔ Guide readers on a "picture walk" through the text by asking them to name the things shown.

✔ Discuss book structure by showing children where text will appear consistently on pages.

✔ Highlight the supportive pattern of the book. Note the consistent number of sentences found on each page.

During Reading

✔ Encourage readers to "read with your finger" and point to each word as it is read. Stop periodically to ask children to point to a specific word in the text.

✔ Reading strategies: When encountering unknown words, prompt readers with encouraging cues such as:

- **Does that word look like a word you already know?**
- **Check the picture.**

After Reading

✔ Write the key words on index cards.

- **Have readers match them to pictures in the book.**
- **Have children sort words by category (words that begin with the letter *c*, for example).**

✔ Ask readers to identify their favorite page in the book. Have them read that page aloud.

✔ Ask children to write their own sentences. Encourage them to use the same pattern found in the book as a model for their writing.

Credits: Cover, © arquiplay77/iStock; 2–3, © David Papazian/Shutterstock; 4–5, © arquiplay77/iStock; 6–7, © monkeybusinessimages/iStock; 8–9, © Yulia Druzenko/iStock; 10–11, © captainsecret/iStock; 12–13, © Sergey Maksienko/Shutterstock; 14–15, © nd3000/Shutterstock; 16T (L to R), © arquiplay77/iStock and © captainsecret/iStock; 16B (L to R), © Sergey Maksienko/Shutterstock, © monkeybusinessimages/iStock, and © Yulia Druzenko/iStock.

Publisher: Kenn Goin   **Senior Editor:** Joyce Tavolacci   **Creative Director:** Spencer Brinker   **Photo Researcher:** Thomas Persano

Library of Congress Cataloging-in-Publication Data in process at time of publication (2019)
Library of Congress Control Number: 2018048657
ISBN-13: 978-1-64280-220-7 (library binding) | ISBN-13: 978-1-64280-393-8 (paperback)